THE SQUANDERED GREEN

Catherine S. Vodrey

2008

East Liverpool, Ohio
www.WordBanquet.com

"On the Way to Nags Head" was previously
published in *Oakland Review*, 1983.

"Thoronet Abbey" was previously published in
Oakland Review, summer 1997.

The author thanks Jim Daniels, Jerry Costanzo,
Hilary Masters and Jean Ferguson Carr of Carnegie
Mellon University and the University of Pittsburgh.

Didn't come up here to read. Came up here to hit.

HENRY AARON

. . . what you once lost—on purpose, by accident—
is delivered to your doorstep sooner or later.
And make no mistake: you are delivered, too,
even to people who'd like to refuse you.
Maybe especially.

ELIZABETH McCRACKEN
Niagara Falls All Over Again

DEDICATION

This is dedicated to my parents,
In honor of their fiftieth wedding anniversary
August 30th, 2008

Jane Green Vodrey
Jackman Stroud Vodrey

Many thanks and love to my husband and kids

Michael Aaron Klein
Henry Jackman Rockwell Vodrey Klein
Lillian Watson Webster Vodrey Klein

Heartfelt thanks to my friend Bill Crawford,
who gets his own page because of his invaluable
and selfless assistance in helping me
design the cover and format the text.

I remain in his debt
and owe him big chockies on an ongoing basis.

Thanks are also due to . . .

Allison Clark Corbett, dearest friend,
fellow label-memorizer and master at Scrabble
and Spite-and-Malice; Bill and Amy Belden,
porch buddies and daiquiri concocters;
Bill Murdock, boon companion on our important
journey; Bridgette Roux Collins, brilliant random
choice by the Carnegie Mellon University housing
department; Clem and Heather O'Donnell, the
best Yars and Iris ever; Dan Corbett, "WageWorks
Spice" and fellow Allison-appreciator; Evie
Zepernick, loving cousin and gentle soul;
Gary Middleton, unswerving confidante
and go-to guy; Katie Hoffman Doman,
separated-at-birth twin; Lee Champeny Bares,
old and dear friend; Lynne and Greg Jones,
who know how to make a game of it;
Mark Miller, who made the whole personal ad
experience completely worthwhile when he
became my buddy; Matt Cullen, host *extraordinaire*
and the one I trust to take care of our Gary;
Sally Watson Cappelli and Helen Vardy Gricks,
dear fellow travelers on the road
since grade school; Sarah Vodrey, sweet sister
and shining example; Tina Hegadorn, wide-world
traveler; Tracy Mangano, sterling friend and
patient listener; William Vodrey, fine brother and
Georges Pompidou reincarnated; and
Zylphia Ford, who came back to Magee
and made him happy, which makes *me* happy.

CONTENTS

TIME IN A BOX

You pass
your metronomic rumor,
Your tale short
And minutely different
Five dozen times an hour.

You will talk to anyone.

We watch your face
In its convex locket,
The frilled corona of Roman lace
You wear to attend
Our waking, our bedtime, the calling of
The exact finish of
What we have to do here.

Your hands knit the hours
To make a day,
Or an age.
You return to us
Our arrogant varnished chart
Of infinity.

Not complicit
With other clocks,
You are independent,
Disdaining truth,
Stand-alone, upright, accurate

Until now
And now
And now.

BOTH OF YOU

Like chlorine, like sweat,
Like shampoo and water,
Your own
Scent is
A fingerprint I know.

I bend my head to yours;
I breathe you in.
Soon you'll pass me,
And breath me in.

PHOTO OF A CIVIL WAR SOLDIER

For Pvt. Oliver Henry
Company F, 61st New York Volunteer Infantry

I am maimed.
It is the first
And most pertinent
Fact about me.
My arm is buried in a Virginia field,
Along with whole and partial
Others.

This was the hand
I learned to write with, the elbow
I injured while threshing, the bicep
That hardened and browned
When I did better work
Than war.

Now my sleeve flaps
Unless I pin it up or my wife
Does, without
Looking me in the eye. It's
A crabbed, flattened salute, almost,
Confirmation that my soldiering has
Stolen from me
My very symmetry, among
Other things.

TULIPS

They announce themselves
With something like
The same tools that planted them:
Spade leaves, little curved trowels
And green marrow knives
Scooping the air to make way
For the pinks and whites that follow.

And when the pinks and whites arrive,
Balloons tethered
To so many slim green lines,
The command of spring will open them
And expose the black brushstrokes,
The trembling stamens,
The gleaming interior
Like the inside of a shell or
An ear, cupped to take in
All it can of the world.

THORONET ABBEY

This is where the nuns hid
Peasants and rebels:
Under their beds.
This is where soldiers strode over
Dozens of twice-captive hearts:
Ribs, then stone slabs.

Fear's hand over their mouths,
Some would cross themselves
And scrape their hands on the protection above.

Sucking the skin
That slowly bloomed red,
They closed their eyes against discovery
While the nuns stood, grouped
In the ancient light of moon,
Modest as swans.

THERE

I was there once—well,
Not there, but a place like there,
A campus, with dorms
And academic buildings
Where people went to classes
And took tests
And ate potato chips in the halls.

I hardly remember
Parts of it: a tiled
Mosaic, minutes and hours of days:
A clock dropped to the floor.

What they will remember
Some time from now
Will be the same, a confetti
Of all of it, but this
One day standing out
With black-lined clarity,
This calamity that strode the halls
And scattered them,
Bent them,
And bends them, still,
To their knees.

SHADOWS

Wherever the moon goes, shadows:
The dark points of the crown
She's flung from the sky.
When we go to bed, she looks down on us from
The east, willing the trees
To bend their forms before her.

When I get up in the middle of the night, I look
Out the window and she's in the west,
The trees' shadows fleeing her as she
Goes down,
Down.

SEAMSTRESS

I've got the world on a string, or at least
This blouse, which I'm mending.

Without the mending, the sleeve hangs
Funny. It came improperly hemmed,
Which is why it was on sale. I thought,
I can fix that.
No big deal.

The inside: a line of loping, irregular stitches.
The outside: tiny pinpricks
No one will see.
What a lovely island of neatness
In this messy world: the surgical dart of metal
Convincing the thread to follow,
In and out,
Up and down,
Pressing the fabric's cheek
To itself, soothing the puckered hem.

Everything is hanging by a thread;
But a thread is
All I need.

WOMEN AND CHILDREN

Think of the *Titanic*
And the rule
That made some men pretend.

Consider the real
Women and children
Who left their real men
On the ship
While they banged their way
Down the hull, lowering
Into a black horizon
Of water and night, a collar
Of foam appearing
As the water rose to accept them.

All around them, like flowers
Loosened from a tossed bouquet,
Were women and children
And men. In the boats,
They bowed their heads:
Against the cold,
Against the view, the floating
People who quieted
After a little while.
They bowed their heads to the god
Who created women and children.

REVERSE

Now I know everything
My parents meant.

I look at you, tall
As some of my friends,
Twice as tall as you were
Half a lifetime ago
And I think that if I could halve you,
Halve the time, the height,
The mistakes we made
Over and over,
Becoming fluent,
(We got them wrong until
We got them right)
If I could get you back to six,
I'd know more, or better,
But I wouldn't.

I'd be thinking
Then, like I know I did then,
That I wanted you to grow up,
Not knowing
Everything my parents meant,
Not hearing them like
You don't hear me.

OUR CIGAR

On that high school
Backpacking trip to Maryland
(Maybe the farthest I'd ever gone
Without my parents),
You and I had our backs to the ground,
Our boots still on,
Roots fingering the ground
Beneath us.

You lit one
For us to share and puffed it
As though you knew
What you were doing;
Maybe you did.

When you passed it to me,
I put my lips to it, I breathed
In, if you could call it that,
And then breathed in further.

You assumed I knew
No one inhales cigars.

I didn't know.

I coughed, you laughed,
We laughed and then laughed harder
When I explained myself.

We wept with laughter
Beneath the stars, beneath our own
Little world of smoke.

THE MIDNIGHT PILLOW

Among friends,
There was a story-writing contest.

You saw your chance.

Out from under your husband's heavy
Name and work,
You slipped with the litheness
Of the teen you were.
His three Y's barely etched
The skin on your back.

That night, on
Your midnight pillow, you
Had a dream, green-tinted
And shadowy.

You knew what terrified you
Would terrify others.
And still (or so)
You began,
Godlike, directing
Your paper doctor to
Set in uneasy, pulsing motion
His handiwork, his patchwork
man made of men.

LIGHT FROM THE WEST

It's golden, so
Golden and clear, that the shadows
It creates respond in kind:
Fuming, delicate,
Wavering and waving,
Smoke on the wall
Of leaves and branches
Not yet burning with color.

I WONDER IF I'LL DIE SLOW OR FAST

I wonder if I'll die slow or fast
As I lie here beneath the desk,
Still,
Waiting for him to leave,
Pretending to be
What he thinks I am.

When was the last time?

Maybe with friends
The summer I was nine
When we played pioneers
And pretended a bear
Had gotten into our cabin.
We knew with a bear:
You played dead.

Never dreaming back then,
Never knowing as I rested on my pine-needle bed,
Comfortable and sweet-smelling,
That someday I'd have to do it
For real, that someday
The bear would be real
And be a man
And have a gun
And point it at me.

HOW IT'S GONE

Since we last met, well,
I got a job, a house, a husband,
Two kids, a dog, a house
For the dog, another job,
Another job, another house
(For us, not the dog) . . .
And you?

Has it been better, different,
Worse, brighter, clearer,
Darker, different?

How would it have been different
For us?

Different
House, jobs, kids, dog,
Different house
For the dog, but the dog
Still noses the air when she smells
A steak on the grill—the dog
Doesn't know this isn't her family.
Do I?

GETTING THE MAIL

Heading down the driveway,
I'm assaulted with light;
The branches are spear tips
Sheathed in ice and sun.
Trees bend to lay down
Their blue rakes on the snow.

On the return, the sun is behind me.
If my children were to walk
Toward me right now, they wouldn't
Recognize me right away,
Haloed as I am from behind,
Face dark,
Blue shadow advancing my cause.

FROM THIS NO ONE IS EXCUSED
For Grace Paley

My parents are standing in the bathroom,
Brushing their teeth together.
My father looks in the mirror and says,
When did Bill Vodrey marry Peg Green?

But here they are:
Instead of my parents, now
It's his father
And her mother, my parents
Apparently having fled along with youth.

They are married and frankly, surprised by it,
Not having chosen each other,
The habits, the annoyances,
The looks they inherited
Each from the other.

The smalltown Ohio boy
And the New Jersey farm beauty
Brush their teeth in silence
And wonder how they met.

FIRST THING

First thing
In the morning,
Just before we actually get up,
I'm awake and hear
The birds
A cocktail party of drunken twits,
Each self-important, talking about the scores,
The recent promotion,
The evil mother-in-law.

What were they drinking?
They are strewn through the trees
As though on a sectional,
Maybe bad-mouthing their host,
Maybe wondering how it got to be so late
It's early.

THE FACT OF IT

It is
Like the air we breathe,
Like the blood that funnels into
The chambered atriums of our hearts
And issues forth again:
Both, the body's necessary habits of
Coalescing with the world.

The fact of it,
Of being on the same planet at
The same time, is
A serendipity and a delight.

Blood like a tide back and forth,
Air winging its way into and out of us,
Perhaps every now and then,
Hearts even beating and breathing
In the same rhythm
At the same instant:
All of this presents
A clasping
That admits neither distance nor time.

It is
A solitary thing knitted of two
Solitary things: each
Of us.

I can find so many things to love
About all of this.

AGREEING ON THE COLORS

What if
It's all a farce,
This agreement we have,
These fingers interwoven
To catch any of us?

And what if
None of us know?

What if we're going along,
Attending to work, children,
Everything in this cup of life,
Anything, really, you can think of,
And what if
While you point to the sky
And say, *Red,*
I'm nodding and laughing?

ALWAYS

Not only permanence,
But plural:
Amplifying whatever
Is yoked to it.

Meaningless until
You attach that S-hook,
That dallying, reversing loop
Like a child's scrawl in the sand,
And suddenly, you have infinity
And solidity and all time and space
Promised to you.

ANY BACH FUGUE

Fulfilling itself like
The cell's strict destiny,
It twins itself, again
And again,
Each new part not new, but original:
Each new part the first.

The cell is one,
Then moments later,
Many, all
Joined together as it unlocks
And fans
An infinite, scalloped array of itself.

This origami unfolding,
This staircase climbing itself,
This open peacock's tail,
This infinitude of mirrors:

It is exactly itself.
It makes perfect and symmetrical sense.
It is how any
God would have done it.

THE APPOINTMENT

The doctor explains:
It could be your body chemistry
Is changing.
It could be your habits:
Diet, sleep, who knows?

Sometimes, he says, *it's not any*
One thing, it's just
The going through it.
I ask what he means.

You know, he says, *the*
Going through it—the passing of time.

The dominoed days, months, years, to find
Yourself here with a new body
That's older, a froth of billions of cells
Laid end to end, a swath of newness
Both microscopic and life-size:
Life's bait-and-switch.

How can I be both new and old?
I'm a philosophical puzzle in a paper gown.
I ask if this is what getting older is.
He deflects the idea of age, and emphasizes
Passage.
Passage through years.
It's a nicer way to think of it,
He says.

ASLEEP

My daughter is asleep. She knows nothing
And cares for nothing
But sleep
When she's asleep.

Later, she will tell me about a dream
In which she rode a lamb across our porch.
I do not see her dreaming now.

The sun experiments on her face:
A roseate band across her forehead,
A smudge of shadow under her chin,
A sickle of light cupping her cheek.

She sleeps as if
This is all she'll ever have to do.

BLACK BIRD

The black bird stands at the edge of the grass:
A period at the end
Of a long green sentence.

He is an emphatic bully in the yard,
Chesting his way around the garden.

His staccato, typewriter-key steps
Are angled and abrupt.

Darting his head to the earth,
He looks as though he's inclined to listen,
As though he can be reasonable, this
Hit man in a sleek black trench,
Plunging death into little
Holes in the earth.

THE BOYS

There are savages in my house:
Six thirteen-year old boys
Warring with foam dart
Guns in our basement.

For just a moment, they don't know
I'm watching, but
I'm watching and I see them
Crouching behind furniture.
Wild animals on the prowl,
Showing themselves briefly
Then hiding again.

I see clearly this march they're on:
Fourteen, fifteen, then
Sixteen and driving,
Eighteen and voting,
Twenty-one and drinking
Or before twenty-one
(Who am I kidding)

And it all starts here, this trip
They're taking to be men, it starts
Here at thirteen, with them
Shooting each other.

BEFORE LIGHT

Only at first
Does it seem still,
Quiet—
But as I lie there
In the middle of the bed
In the middle of the room,
Industry abounds.

There is the ant traversing
The country of kitchen tile;
There is the dog dragging
A deer leg under our deck;
There is my daughter
Choosing what shirt
Will make the boy she likes
Look.

My body is perfectly still
As I look down at it,
But inside, I know
That there are
Coiled highways
And factories,
This country I own
But will never see.

Everything inside me is
The blue and the red,
The to and fro,

The call and response of
Blood and oxygen
Convincing the engine inside me,
Go on,
Go on,
And my heart
Agreeing.

THE CREEK IS FROZEN

The creek is frozen, or nearly
Frozen, all of it, except
A narrow slash of moving water
Grey and diagonal against the white,
A correction on a page.

DUKE AND TEDDY

Next door to us
Live Duke and Teddy
And Peggy and Precious.

Peggy and Precious
Are the woman and the cat:
This we know.

Duke and Teddy
Are the man and the dog, or
The dog and the man:
We can never remember.

When they pass our house
On their afternoon walk,
We call out,
Hey Duke,
Hey Teddy.
Not wanting to mistake
One for the other
So they never know.

We think Duke is the man,
But either way.

The man tells us about the Pirates
And their chances.

Probably no pennant this year,
But maybe next year.

The dog tells us nothing,
But we think he knows
We don't know.

Peggy comes out onto the porch
In her housecoat,
Shapeless woman in her
Shapeless clothes, calling longingly,
Her creaky voice
Unhinging: *Precious,*
Precious.

THE ECLIPSE

It couldn't have been colder;
The moon was a promise
Of light and heat
That would never be kept.

We were sitting on the floor,
Looking out the window.

The binoculars sharpened the moon
To a thin foreign coin,
Then a cookie with a nibble,
Then a paring of apple or cheese,
Then half of a pair
Of parentheses.

The eclipse was a tired hand,
Slowly, slowly
Wiping the moon's forehead.

It smudged
The moon into a ghost.
The stars brightened.

UPON ARRIVAL

He cried: the first miracle.

The second: you shaded
His eyes from the light and
He stopped.

Fists fierce
With such rounded determination
You'd think he knew
He held the world.

TOOLS
For Jim Daniels

It's all right there:
Twenty-six and change,
The letters and all the marks
That make meaning bloom and color
Any pen-and-ink sketch.

The demure comma,
Its little hem finishing the edge
Of the clause.

The period like the pointed
End of a finger.

Dashes—stitches racing to attach
One thought to the next.

The question mark
Bends its head back towards
The sentence:
Did you really mean to say that?

And the exclamation point,
Tarnished with overuse
According to a college professor
Of mine, who admonished
Against its pogo stick bounce,
Its buoyant charisma.

We argued about it once, he and I.
So I turned in a short story
In which I'd created a burning house,
A box filled with horrifying heat,
Paned with hellish windows,
And I made the characters
Gaze upon it while saying,
Fire,
Fire.

VIRGINIA WOOLF IN HER GARDEN

The war began and we moved,
Leonard and I, to the country
To escape the danger, the searing drone
Of the bombers, the jittery sense
That death would gladly
Meet us in the streets.

The country is no safer.
Air war travels anywhere
It wants.

My foxgloves
Spear the air, their frilled cups
Inviting bees, and so I imagine
I hear bees
But only for a moment
Before I realize it's
Them overhead,
Stylized spiders under each wing,
The Germans, paying us no
Attention at all as they usher
Death to the cities.

CYST

When she was twenty,
She went to the doctor.
My back is bothering me,
She said.
There's this spot.

He examined her and found
It, the tender, spongy mass
That insisted back
When pressed.

A minor surgery
And the cyst was removed.

To be sure, they do
Tests. They ask the thing
What it is
And they believe it.

The cyst offered up these
Occult responses:
Hair, material of bones
And fingernails.

She had been one of two:
A twin now singled out.
The egg she'd been had overcome
The other

As one overcomes trouble
Or grief.

She imagined the thing in reverse:
Nestled against the unknown
Sister, two microscopic peas in a pod.
Herself
And the sister as the two devolved
Into one; first growth,
Then assumption.

Sometimes there are teeth,
The doctor told her.

YOUR NAME

I write it on envelopes
as direction,
the neat map
that gets my words from here to there.

At night,
before sleep has clasped me to darkness,
I move my mouth to say it,
feeling this silent chant
in a still hour
could make your face appear.

Anything is possible.
I believe in this.

When it doesn't work,
I know what to expect.
I go on writing your name,
speaking your name
and my name with it,
two fingers crossing for luck.

A MOTHER WEEPS AT TWO GRAVES

Here,
Where humanity has apparently left
All humans, where around us, men have
Devolved, devolved—
I don't know another word for it
Or for this.

Here, where
My children,
My children,
Two of them—
It takes my breath away.

Let me start again.
I have to say it.

I cannot tell you the whole story.

My children
Lie still
Beneath my feet.
It takes my breath away
To know people can walk
Over them, will walk
Over them.

With fearsome, everyday power
We made two children.
One and a half years of my life

Creating two hearts and minds.
Each one knitted together
Of two: their father and me,
Each one constructed
Of blood and time.

They now
Are stopped clocks.
A mother is not meant to see
That her children are finite.

No,
No.

UNDERSTANDING THE VIOLETS

I take the camera out in the woods
And I use it to witness
All the purple beauty.
I try not to intrude;
I just want to capture.
But I'm not above removing
The diagonal stick.

I used to stand over the violets,
Camera eyeing down,
My universal view—
Is this what God saw
After He decided on purple?

This time, I decide to crouch,
And then lie down.
I am on my stomach,
Chin and elbows a tripod.
I am among the violets,
Of them,
Aswim in the purpled grassy sea.
I focus, I snap.

Somewhere in there,
I hold my breath.

THAT TRACK MEET

They're at the reunion, together
After fifty years of not.
Talking over
The voices around them
And the old days.
Remember? the engine for every sentence,
Aah, boy and *Oh, it was great.*
Remember?

Someone brings up that track meet,
The one in Durham, the one
Where some wiseass snitched
The starter pistol. He had an idea:
Kick up a little dust in this backwater.

They had the big black limo, the one
My dad borrowed from his grandfather.

They drove it to the middle of town.
One of them pretended
To saunter down the street,
One of them had the starter pistol, and
The rest lay in wait in the limo.

Pistol darted out, pretended
To shoot Saunter, who pretended
To fall down dead on the sidewalk
While the rest of them swarmed out of
The limo, beetles out of a black husk,

Picked up the body, threw it in the trunk, and
Screeched out of town in a hurry.

People froze on the sidewalks.

My mother,
Who has heard all the stories,
Can't believe she's never heard this one
And is admiring. My father is enjoying it,
Nodding, laughing. He knows
It was a good one.

STARTING THE FIRE

After a stutter-start,
The match performs
Its magic trick:
Finding fire in the air.

My son touches the flame to
The newspaper, where it
Brightens, then darkens
News of the world.

SPRING, DECEMBER

Bird's-eye view:
We are surrounded by snow.
It heaps and mounds in every city
North, south, east, west
Of us.

We alone remain unwhite.

We are green, in fact,
The lilacs obliged to bud
By the agreement they have with
The air, the sun,
This lie of spring
In December.

RECOGNITION

I didn't know what I had.

You name it,
I failed to recognize it.

There were things I gave away
With both hands
That I've give anything for now.

Eager, on to the next thing,
Always pinning my hopes
On some lapel I'd glimpsed in the dark.

Now I know.

THE MINK

Even though I've never seen you
Before, I know
Immediately
What you are.

You dart your sleek head
Out of the underbrush,
And then you're a
Mercury ripple across the grass,
Like you're swimming
Or fluid yourself.

HOW TO REMEMBER

You told me
That kings play chess on fat girls' stomachs.
I never before could remember
Kingdom, phylum, class, order,
Family, genus, species.

I picture the kings on a beach,
A conference of sovereigns
Barefoot on the sand.

They wear their robes:
Ermine, wine-colored velvet,
Embroidered bees and fleurs-de-lis.

The air is hot.
The kings are seated
Or reclining, ample
Nude girls spread before them
Like a buffet. The girls lie still,
Eyes closed against the sun rising
Over the blue horizon,
Knowing the game is long,
Knowing they may end the day
With a negative
pawn-shaped burn.

FIRST WALK

It is the first walk I have taken
This spring, on March 21st,
The arbitrary first day.

If I wait for the mood to strike,
I'll never move, so I move and
The mood follows.

I set out to see the state line,
The border of paved to
Not-so-paved,
Forty-five minutes each way
And a big hill for my exercise.

The roadside daffodils
Raise their little yellow clamor
And sway with each passing car.

ENDINGS

My father always called it "the Mack truck."
But it could be anything:
The vein with the sheer, glistening bubble,
The sixth bourbon,
The ice on the step,
The burglary gone wrong,
The congenital condition
No doctor saw.

Whether it's the truck or the stroke,
What we earn or inherit,
Whatever precedes the identical end
And the unanimous black is
Our last individual act to suffer
Or employ.

ON THE SONOGRAM

I am a locket.
Open me up, and
There I am:
Entire and perfect.
Concocted in
a dark and miniature genesis,
Everything I am
unfurling from
A spine of seed pearls.

EMPTYING THE ASHES

Such a noisy removal
Of something so entirely silent.

The chatter that arises
As the tools meet each other,
And the andirons, and the holder
That cradles the logs
From the initial flare
To the hot demise.

We shovel the ashes into a paper bag
And take them outside
To scatter them in the woods:
Trees to feed trees.

BEJEWELED

It is unseasonably cold and
I am biking through the woods.
Exhilarated by the wind in my face,
The unexpected snowflakes,
The bright, bitter air in my lungs,
I surge.

Not there, then instantly
There,
A branch, thorned,
Slender, plum-frosted.

The part of my brain that's
Hundreds of thousands of years old
Knows to arrow out my arm, to grab it,
To keep it from my eyes.

But I let go too soon and the branch
Returns, whip-thin,
With one thorn in the perfect spot,
Set like a high, small
Crown, a pronged setting
Lacking only a gemstone.

All of this in an instant: it snaps forward,
Kisses me, whips
Back and I have already surged,
The bike's wheels racing ahead.

For just a moment, I don't realize the kiss,
Can't feel the blood bead
Bejeweling the groove of my lip.

AT THE CAR WASH

He is patient with me,
This man with about five teeth in his head,
As he explains once again
About the spray wax.
You can see through it,
He says, *It won't cloud the windshield*
Because glass is slippery and
The wax rolls right off it.
It only clings to the body of the car
Because the paint has little, tiny pores all over.
Gives the wax something to grip, he says.
I promise, he says.

The next day, driving in the rain,
I see what he means;
The windshield is clear, the wipers
Are ticking back and forth,
And I can see fine.
I can see the raindrops on the hood,
Thousands of them
Trembling and clinging,
Bulging at the turns, clinging still
So as not to lose their grip and slide off.

Like all of us,
I think.

THANKS FOR LETTING ME KNOW

Ignore it,
My mother said when a mean boy
Tortured me with remarks.
Ignore it and he'll stop.
He only wants the reaction.

He didn't stop. One day
When I was seven or eight,
I hit him upside the head
With a white patent leather purse
I'd filled with rocks.
He left me alone after that.

Now my daughter has a bully:
An ex-friend.
She's weepy about it.
I don't recommend the purse method.
But I tell her,
We'll practice.
We'll practice what to say.

So in the car on the way to school,
I say to her, *That's an ugly shirt.*
In the back seat she sings out,
Thanks for letting me know.
You're stupid, I say.
Sorry you're feeling so crabby today,
Says my righteous daughter.

I cringe to introduce her
To these insults I'm speaking
As though they're realities.

But I'm trying to arm her
With something more than a purse
Filled with rocks.

ON THE WAY TO NAGS HEAD

The bridge sings,
Movement thrumming it
Into a long, gleaming note.

August always pulls us here
To the Atlantic,
To the days of tyrannical light
To the high moon,
A quivering rickrack on the water.

HANGING IT UP

Most cool nights,
I wear my grandfather's cardigan:
The tarnished buttons,
Loden trim,
Grey pebbled wool,
Something he bought in Vienna
Or Bavaria
On one of many trips.

For a long time,
It smelled like him, or
I just imagined that it did:
Smoke and must and mildew
And hay dust from the horsebarn.

Now it smells like my day
And I air it out—hanging it up
Each evening on the back
Of the bedroom chair.

It has passed through
The woodland air and spores
Are caught in it.
It has passed through
The city air with its
Gas and sulfur.
It has passed through
An evening at home,

Of watching television,
Of reading Dahl or Colwin,

An evening of mail and dinner
And talk of maybe
Going to Vienna.

THE DAY THE HAWK FLEW DOWN

There were the boys, teenagers,
Just,
Out on the field, all of them with
Legs springy and loose, and
There was the pitcher,
His arm gangly, lengthy,
Wonderfully knit of muscle
And bone, a good
Pitching arm.

So he pitched and
The batter hit it and
They watched the ball rise
Like hope or the sun,
When into that eternal blue
With its lone white planet
Flew a hawk,
A kestrel, maybe, small
And fast like a bullet
Is small and fast.
Then the kestrel aimed its claws
Before it: delicate, almost, careful,
Exact, the way you would if
You were picking up a winking
Shard of glass.

It seized the ball
With the blank confidence and surety

Bred in it by the ages
And it rode the ball

To the ground, rode it down
The swooping, sudden, miraculous
Silence of the crowd.

CREATION

The homeliest of nests:
A bed.
And us in it,
Unclothed, unguarded, asplay
With intent and desire.

A trillionth of you meets
A trillionth of me:
Creation unpleats its
Spiral staircase to fill
Me with us, or a combination
Of us: a new two-in-one.

Heart, brain, organs,
The vague marble eye unseeing
The thumb it sucks, the tailbone still
Tail, the knees folded to chin
We will kiss
Upon arrival.

THE PORTRAIT

It is a kind of egg—a capsule
Holding all the world
In a tiny space.
My great-grandmother
Painted my grandmother
When she was pregnant with
My mother.

Here is the plumb line of descent:
Three generations pulled, one
Down to the next.

Here we all are: my great-grandmother
At the canvas, hair unfussed-over,
Brushes working a lattice
Of color.

My grandmother in her
Russet dress begins to appear:
She is seated
On a kingly chair, knitting:
Perhaps something for the baby.
She looks down at her work,
At her expert fingers.

My mother is hidden,
Undisturbed. I am nowhere,
Unimagined yet, but
I hear the clock.

ON THE EARTH

I lie here in the grass
Back pressed to the same earth
That holds everyone else
On earth.

What a feeling:
To be on the earth itself,
Not a floor, a rug, a chair,
But the earth alone,
Nothing between me and this entire planet,
Its orbit braceleting the sun.

THE FIRST KISSES

It was something
Like spin-the-bottle, but it was something
Else. No parents. We played it
In the TV room of Jackie's house.

You took me out into the hall
And you kissed me
For real, and I was
Initiated into something big:
I knew it.
When you kissed Jackie later, jealousy
Made its sinuous red journey
Up my spine.

* * *

We were standing under a drainpipe outside
As a party churned chaos inside.
None of us were supposed to be there.

The moon was over your head,
And I looked at it
Instead of you
When I took this thought
Out of my head and gave it air:
Kiss me.
To my amazement, you bent
And kissed me.
I was fifteen

And had never seriously considered
That simply asking could get me
What I wanted.

* * *

You were my sister's friend—a tanned
Boy with good looks and a smile
That was slow and meaningful.

You liked me back.
We went for a walk
Out onto the swinging bridge
Over the creek's
Constant journey.

In the very center
Of it—you balanced
And me balanced before you—
You leaned in and I did, too,
We unbalanced and met
In that lovely center: the middle of the bridge
In the middle of the afternoon
In the middle of a kiss.

* * *

I decided I needed a boyfriend. I was
Sixteen and loud: too much trouble
For any reasonable boy.
So I picked you,

As dramatic and opinionated
As I was.
As long as all we did was kiss,
We were fine.

* * *

You were outside my bedroom window:
Innocent, though,
In the sun, painting the shutters.
It wasn't what it could have been
In my feverish teenaged head.

You didn't know it, but you fanned
That fever when you talked with me
Through the screen.
Amiable and funny,
Your Outer Banks accent was
A balm and a trick.

Over the next three weeks, we went
To a couple of movies, spent
A couple of evenings talking on the porch.
One night you said, *Let's sit*
On the sand tonight and look
At the moon.
Which we did. You used
The light to see me
And to find my lips
And kiss me:
The best use for moonlight.

* * *

I had a crush on you.
Then I lived in Spain
For the summer
And my crush dissipated.

When I returned, we were in college
Together, starting out,
New college friends after
Having been old high school friends.

You had a crush on me.
Our cross-purposed attraction
Was a frustration and so we decided
To try it, to reverse our bad timing:
To kiss.

And who knows why, but we kissed
In the middle of Forbes Avenue
On a Saturday night, traffic
Streaming around us, headlights
Weaving the night. We kissed

And we laughed and we ran
For the curb
As the light changed.

* * *

You were my only really tall boyfriend,
With a wonderful made-for-stage-and-screen
Real name.
You dressed as Dracula for the party;
I was your blushing victim.
Feeling dainty was a foreign experience
I welcomed.

* * *

You told me you were the grandson
And namesake
Of the actor who played the Lone Ranger on TV.
Who knows if it was true, but
What fun to believe.
We sat in your car and talked
And talked and talked, my God,
When all I wanted to do was kiss.

* * *

After the party,
You walked me to my dorm.
You were in the hall while I stood
Just inside my room.
Between us was the threshold.
Behind you was light;
Behind me was darkness.
I knew, I knew
You were going to kiss me but
I loved the wait

And leaned in only reluctantly
At the very edge of it,
Stepping over into new territory
With this slender passport.

* * *

I don't remember the first one. But this
I remember: standing in your mother's kitchen
While you snitched raisins she was macerating
For rum raisin ice cream.
You ate them and then kissed me.

* * *

We were a picture postcard,
The two of us:
Beach,
Ocean,
Sunset,
Kiss.

* * *

You were my friend's ex.
This was against the rules.
I knew the rules, but
We were all alone.
You liked my pale green silk shirt
And when you told me so
And I hugged you,

You kissed me. A fair trade
For a compliment. Then
We sat on the porch and kissed
And kissed, the street light
An available moon.

* * *

The room was a black hole.
We were in sleeping bags on the floor,
Having thought it would be fun
To sleep in front of the fire.

We forgot fires go out.

And it did go out. You were hesitant
In the best possible way—the way
That expands the compass
Of all possibilities. In that dark,
We found each other's faces anyway
And kissed.

I pretended
I could see.

GOOSE

Since you travel in flocks, it's hard
To see only one of you.
But I try.

The mask that covers your face
And scarves your throat,
The onyx beak,
The white chin strap,
The pellet eye: stylized beauty at odds
With your teenage boy voice,
Each awkward high note
Strangled by a lower one.

STRAWBERRIES

We didn't tell you
A baby was coming.
We wanted you
To figure it out.
A little game of ours: to see
How long it took you.

When you finally asked,
I was six months along,
My awkward bulk ahead of me
Like life.

One day
You patted me and in a patient voice
Asked, *Where's the baby?*

I said she wasn't here yet—that
She needed more time.

She'll come when she's ripe?
You asked and I thought
Of apples, pears, especially strawberries
With their one
Really good day, their perfect
Ripeness that lasts only
One sun's pass across the sky
And I thought of the stain they leave
On your tongue and how

You love them and how
There would be another stained tongue
When we eat strawberries next.

FROZEN PIPES

I'm alone in the house when I hear it:
A sudden hailstorm, or a metal box
Dragging across concrete. I can't
Find it, I can't
Figure it out. I finally
Go to the bathroom and pause at
The door, afraid to
Open it, afraid not to
Open it,
Hearing the audience yelling,
Don't touch that door!

FOR MY MOTHER

1984

I have been walking towards you
All of my life.

In photographs of us as children,
A generation spreads its arms
In the space between
Black-and-white and color.

My years are perforated
With small rebellions:
Cigarettes and other efforts
To scratch out a line between us.

Did you know
Twenty-two years ago
That the new name rising beneath your hands
Would wear your face?

Did you know that on certain warm nights
My father would hear a laugh on the porch
And would waver, uncertain,
In the half-light of the kitchen
To wonder which of us
Was happy?

CAT NAMES

Our daughter presents it
As a once-in-a-lifetime opportunity:
Our chance to own
A cat—*To go with*
The dog, she says.
A natural pairing.

She makes a list
Of names.
Girl names: April,
Petra, Meredith, Mouse
(she thinks this is a fine joke).
Boy names: Ringo, Nemo,
Amos, Ian.

At the bottom, she writes:
Well?
And
Kitty name finally decided:
Then a long line
For us to fill in
Our decision.

THE FISHING SPIDER

I'm sweeping the front step,
Minding my own business,
When I lift up the mat
And shriek.

The largest spider I've ever seen
Is under the mat, tensed
And ready
To run up the sill and into the house
Which it does.

Even my spider-admiring husband
Is awed when he comes running
Towards my shriek and sees
The monster king spider
Of all spiders.

I got it, I got it, he says as he
Doesn't get it.

But finally in it goes, down the metal sides
Of an old coffee can, and sits at the bottom
Like an intaglio, feet touching
The sides,
If you can believe it.

We look it up.
We live in the woods and
Have all the books. It is a

Fishing spider, which means
It doesn't bother with insects,
But dines instead on actual fish,
Which it catches because it stays
Underwater
For half an hour at a time.

We all shiver
And wonder
How much our toes look
Like minnows.

ON THE EXECUTION
OF SADDAM HUSSEIN

What an insult!

The body you were born with,
The only thing any of us really know
Intimately
Conspires with gravity
Waiting,
Invisible hands cupped
Beneath the trapdoor.

APRIL 3rd

How is it
That on April third,
there is snow all over the ground,
And a ladybug inside the window?

The window is fogged with the push-pull
Of warm inside and cold outside.

Garnet gem-button,
The ladybug tracks a drunken doodle
On the fogged glass
With her tiny feet.

Does she have a plan?
Does she have a destination?

If I keep her inside, she'll die.
If I open the window, she'll die,
Rose red on snow white.

ON THE PORCH LATE THAT NIGHT

It was a celebration
Of how long we'd been
Us and how long all of us
Had been friends.
We raised laughter and drinks
Together in the dark.
Our voices were pebbles thrown
Against night's great, broad back.

It was darkened, but not
Dark, the candle flames just
Little volunteer flags,
Hapless in the occasional breeze,
So easily swayed.

We stayed,
None of us
Wanting to end it, none of us
Wanting to come in and so
The night stretched itself from evening
To night to very early morning.
Unreasonable, really—aren't we all
Too old to be doing this?

But we did it, we laughed
And talked; we frittered our time
Away that night, a trove of hours
We plundered.

We were gluttonous.
We were a bracelet,

Each of us linking to the next,
Each of us with our backs to the night,
Our faces turned inward, looking
At each other, looking into that light,
Ignoring
What might be outside
While we warmed ourselves
At the center of it all.

CHANGE

It's all different every minute,
It's all change,
Coins in a pocket
Different music every time you make
A purchase or ask
For change.

Some of the changes amount to loss.

And as time goes on,
As it does every second,
We are diminished.
We are that universal: the period
At the end of the sentence.

THE BEACHED WHALE

What if
They hadn't formed a net
Of their hands
To push her out to sea?

What if instead,
They had left her
A hulking new boulder
On the beach?

What if
Nothing had moved her?

Years from now,
After time had frayed the skin
And sea birds had made a banquet
Of what was underneath,
The fence of bones would stand.

The whale would mark
Her own grave
Neatly, magnificently,
Her ribs stitching together
The seamed horizon:
Sky to water.

THE RATTAN COUCH

Who knows why we are moving it,
But we are moving it
From one place to the other.

My father straps it on top of the station wagon.
My father, who won't let anyone else
Pack the car or strap the couch
Or set anything into place:
Because no one will do it right.

We all get in. My sister and brother and I
Are crammed into the back seat,
Legs sticking to the vinyl, complaining
As we listen to the Pirates game on the radio.
My mother shushes us
So we can hear the score.
My father says as he pulls out, *Don't let me*
Forget about the couch. Don't let me
Forget it's on top of the car.

There is some important, senseless thing
We decide to argue about in the back seat.
We argue with vigor and self-righteousness
And loud voices—so loud, in fact,
That my parents get involved,
Reminding us of all the *blah blah blah* about
Not saying anything at all
If we can't be nice.

The garage looms. I think
You know what happens next.
None of us have ever heard such a terrific
Crunching sound: the creaking, screeching
Riot of a couch devolving
Into lumber.

My father is furious. We laugh so hard
It hurts. It's a good one:
Seeing the smartest man we know
Participate in the slapstick, mindless
Destruction of a perfectly good couch.

It may be
The most fun we've had all summer.

MAPLES IN AUTUMN, FREDERICKTOWN

Durable above the swale,
It loosens bits of seeded veil.
Maples simplified to wisps,
Breeze-encradled, veer and list.

Not only seeds are disengaged,
But leaves depart the branching cage.
Resting earthbound, each defies
The reason of the viewing eye.

Leaves, no, but this beneath the heel:
Sunlight, blood, and citrus peel.
Summer's squandered green now turns
In autumn's kiln and lit there, burns.

A SHORT HISTORY OF JACK AND JANE

Here you have my parents' first impressions of each other:

My father: "I thought she was a good sport."
My mother: "I thought he looked like a bug."

They met at Princeton University, where my father was a student and where my mother was with her parents visiting friends. Both my grandfathers were in the class of 1926 at Princeton, although they didn't know each other. On that hot day in May 1958, my father—wearing the reflective aviator sunglasses that gave rise to the insect impression—spotted my mother, decided she was a looker, and asked her to join him in playing volleyball. My mother accepted.

The volleyball game went well enough that my father—starved for female company in that all-male enclave—said, "Hey, my parents just gave me a bunch of tickets to Broadway shows. Want to go with me?" It was the era of "West Side Story," "Carousel," and "The Music Man." My mother was thrilled at the opportunity to gorge on theatre. The boy asking was nice enough. Why not?

Why not? Because my mother was engaged. Her fiancé was still in Europe, from whence she'd recently returned. Because he had a military commitment to honor, they'd agreed that upon her return to the States, they could each go out with other people—in, you know, an above-board manner, for things like coffee and movies. No harm could come of it. It was a way of killing time until he returned and they could marry.

So my mother and father went from the Princeton volleyball game to dinner to something else to somewhere else. The casual coffee-or-movies set-up had been transformed into a real live date.

My mother had a longstanding policy of never kissing on the first date. But as she explained to me years later, "I kissed your father on the first date because it was such a *long* first date." All of the sudden, it was well after midnight and my mother figured the whole thing was roughly the equivalent of three or four dates, so really, when you looked at it that way, you could almost say that my father was due a kiss or four.

Over the next couple of weeks, my parents went to half a dozen Broadway shows courtesy of my grandparents' birthday tickets. At the end of this time, my father proposed to my mother in her father's car as they tried to wait out a driving rainstorm. She giggled and said, "Oh, Jack, you're such a kidder," never stopping to consider that any reasonable person could hang such a momentous question on such a slender new thread.

He got angry; she burst into tears. He slammed a door in her face; she drove home. She walked into her parents' home crying, and said to her father, "I think Jack just proposed to me."

My mother proceeded to break the engagement seven times. She decided to go through with it only once the engraved invitations had arrived. In a weird inversion of practicality and romanticism, her lifelong Depression-bred aversion to waste led her to reason that it would be terrible to squander an expensive item which had only one possible use.

And so on a hot day at the end of August, fifty years ago, my parents married in a church in Elizabeth, New Jersey. They had known each other a whopping three months. The photographs show them to look, as most bridal couples do, hopeful and delighted and—perhaps—a little shocked. My mother is gowned in a very simple floor-length silk dress of her own making, and she is wearing the antique family veil from 1859. In several photographs, her head is thrown back with laughter, her smile offered up to the heavenly blue above. She coyly lifts the hem of her gown a little to show the camera her bare feet as she stands on the grass in her parents' yard.

My father, in all the photographs, looks about seventeen years old. They know each other so remotely, so little, that when my mother offers my father a bite of the wedding cake—fruitcake, as was traditional in her family—he recoils as though she'd produced a live snake. He hates all fruitcake and won't eat it. She doesn't know this, like so much she doesn't know.

Their blind, foolish leap into the forever of matrimony rests on these narrow slats: they make each other laugh. They like kissing each other. They are both cradle Episcopalians and children of the Princeton Class of 1926. Perhaps you could throw in that they are both tall, that they both have dark eyes and dark hair.

That doesn't count for much; none of it does. And yet these spokes are enough to make the wheel of their marriage turn. Eleven months after the wedding, my sister is born. I arrive a couple of years later and my brother a couple of years after that. Over the years, there are dogs, bikes, school, station wagons, and guinea pigs. There are Christmas trees and family vacations and sleepovers in the basement. There is the move back to my father's hometown in eastern Ohio, and there is the busy family life in the big stone house my great-grandfather had built in 1909.

There are skids and sideswipes and near-misses throughout the decades. As I begin to formulate my own ideas on marriage, I think to myself, "I guess it works for them, but I wouldn't have it." So much is resting on so little. Even in my childhood, there are times when I think, "These people don't know each other!" There are times when I don't understand what's going on between them. But I come to learn, eventually, that it's not up to me to understand; they understand, and they are the ones in the marriage.

Marriage is neatly composed of so many dovetailed pairs: the husband and the wife, the public and the private, the shimmering moments and the grinding drudgery. Of course in my youth, I don't understand this. I only know what I see and I am seeing only half—or far less than that, even— of all the pairs of things that click into place to form the larger structure of their marriage.

I know everything, as we all do when we're young. I feel qualified to judge my parents' marriage, and I do so constantly. I am scornful, at times, of what I see as their provincial arrangement. My marriage, if I ever bother to get married, will be free of pettiness and boredom and filled with complete understanding and laughter and excitement and romance and little twittering birds flitting about in the corners.

I promise myself that if I have kids, I will never stay home full-time with them (except that I will); I will write novels and be an actress and possibly a spy (except that I won't).

Eventually, I do marry. As with all marriages, ours has both shimmering moments and grinding drudgery. The passage of time has helped transform my attitude from one of judging to one of feeling humbled. Having faced some marital difficulties a few years back has tempered my outlook as well. I have watched the disintegration of friends' marriages, and the hollow, sleeping march of marriages which might have been better ended —or never begun. But what do I know. What I know is this, above all else: no one really knows what goes on in a marriage except the two people who are in it.

The good sport and the bug are about to celebrate fifty years together. My parents decided to stand together on what could have been quicksand but turns out to have been bedrock. There is luck and serendipity in what they have done, but there is also a shared ability to see something no one else saw, and to see it early and truly.

They know it means something big, this half-century mark. They will celebrate it. But on some foundational level, they can't take it in—they can't process it. After all, they are only twenty-three years old. They barely know each other, and they certainly don't know what they're doing. They're crazy! They're in love. It's the same thing.

A FEW NOTES

The font used for this volume is Corbel.

The cover photograph depicts a cut hyacinth stem in an amethyst vase filled with water. It was taken by the author with a Canon EOS 40D digital camera. The author photograph was taken by Henry J. R. V. Klein.

ABOUT THE AUTHOR

Catherine S. Vodrey is a graduate of Shady Side
Academy, Carnegie Mellon University and
Duquesne University.

She is the author of *A Centennial History of the Hall
China Company*. Her writing, photographs and
recipes have been published in a number of
magazines, including *American Heritage, Better
Homes & Gardens, Cincinnati Magazine, Country
Home, Gourmet,* and *The Old Farmer's Almanac.*

Vodrey is a contributing author to *The
Encyclopedia of Appalachia*. Her web site,
www.WordBanquet.com, features a broad
overview of her work.

This is her first volume of poetry. She lives in the
woods of eastern Ohio with her family.

www.ingramcontent.com/pod-product-compliance
Lightning Source LLC
Chambersburg PA
CBHW031901090426
42741CB00005B/589